Textu

D1602774

Also by Fady Joudah

POETRY

Alight

The Earth in the Attic

TRANSLATIONS

Like a Straw Bird It Follows Me
    (poems by Ghassan Zaqtan)

If I Were Another (poems by Mahmoud Darwish)

The Butterfly's Burden (poems by Mahmoud Darwish)

Textu

Fady Joudah

Copper Canyon Press

Printed in the United States of America

Copper Canyon Press is in residence at Fort Worden State Park in Port Townsend, Washington, under the auspices of Centrum. Centrum is a gathering place for artists and creative thinkers from around the world, students of all ages and backgrounds, and audiences seeking extraordinary cultural enrichment.

"The Old Man Who Wept" appeared in *New Humanist* magazine.

library of congress cataloging-in-publication data

Joudah, Fady, 1971–
  [Poems. Selections]
  Textu / Fady Joudah.
      pages cm

  ISBN 978-1-55659-476-2 (pbk.)
  I. Title.

  PS3610.O679A6 2014
  811'.6—dc23

                                        2014031838
98765432 first printing

Copper Canyon Press
Post Office Box 271
Port Townsend, Washington 98368
www.coppercanyonpress.org

for Hana

Contents

The TEXTU

All the poems here were composed on a cellular phone's text-message screen. The Textu poem has only one hard rule: that it be exactly 160 characters long, specific to text-message parameters. The Textu poem also suggests a meter in character, not syllable, count.

Immune

My heart isn't another's
love is no transplant

it can be
or when I'm dead

I will give you my eyes & also my liver
you must suppress their memory of me

Commissure

Where your lips seem to end
small mouth

they extend & flutter
then dip into your dimpling cheeks!

In that marionette valley
I want to rest my lips

Descending Tongue

I am a fig of your imagination
fig meant for it

you'll care a fig
give a fig bleach it

my flesh is red my milk white
my skin is honey sweat

Iron Maiden

we're in the no reply zone
Still I will bang my body

into your body's rhythms
We know God is OK with us

touching jamming
silence with our breaths

Bulb

My cyanide love in the pit
you underestimate

the vibe of bulbs in your dermis
I am wave you are kelp

not ninja in bamboo forest!
We are gardener & tulip

Eurydice

Low visibility midsummer fog
you are deaf cold your eyes

a grasshopper statute
of limitations on return

Now you are declassified
it is about to snow

Ariadne

Your thread an odyssey in space
institution's eyes had subsidized

before they left you you
became Sufi your God

spun you you
hanging there spun back!

A Thousand & One Nights

Surely Penelope had sex
in her husband's absence

With slave men & women
the undocumented

Folks in other words
the blind could not see

Divorce

Persephone your yearly sabbatical
was always brief & forced

You couldn't begin or end a book
yet you wrote

"Not Catholic & more
stunning than Azrael"

Because

no touch no lover
except in the mirror

neuron all lovers betray all lovers
pray to the mirror

someone's singing in the shower
glass of glass of glass

They

lost each other in the war
he fled with the kids to the border

two years later
she made it to the refugee camp

he'd remarried
she became the second wife

The husband was a pharmacist
the multilingual doctor who delivered the news

was laughing
the worst catastrophe he said

makes you laugh
I never met the wives

The doctor would die later on
from an unknown illness

he knew what it was
the risk of stigma & loss

of income a brilliant clinician he was
for him death was

a thing that happens
As if a country I had

been building had come
crashing in a single life his life

Not country exactly but lots of small lives
Mr. Measure

Doc took photos seriously
unlike us in the predestined world

our spontaneous poses
he posed

as if his full being depended on it
as if it were a silent movie

Discipline & Punish

Zeus the 1st photographer
often using flash

documenting the world
bearing witness

It's not his forms so much
as his high-tech criminality

Do You Remember

that night the war ended
our weapons your war

the camp's clinic was burned to the ground
our clinic your health

what had you secure-
ly there

Those who remain are

those who are maimed
the poem worked its fingers through your
bones

Economy of charity
a lending being lent

your distance
away from here

The Chosen

There's no ram inside me
to offer to a place

every morning is imaginary
& every people is invented

A woman kissed is not a woman
in a kiss kissing

Chronic

Caterpillar you will not become butterfly
or vanish into light

vision will not seduce you or flight
you are siege

a ravishing ravaging
war & medicine

A Childhood

So many kites a school
of jellyfish floating

hide & seek with tanks in the streets
no Tomahawk in Apacheless sky

no snipers or curfew
on rooftops

I sift through clouds

to find you & through grain
through rice & lentils you were

the wholesome one
who holds no simile no form

you are ever-changing
& done!

Honeycomb

Wisdom comes late
a pomegranate's caviar womb

Penicillin kills what kills what kills
as a cat chases its tail

& an infant
tracks shadow like a wolf

Revolution 1

The proof's in the putting
the back nine isn't like the front

Do I know what democracy is
watching another seek it

Amazing grace
sweet toothache

Revolution 2

Imagine we desisted to vote
where & when we could

how would the poem proceed?
You'd say

we'd be asking for water to die
But you Sir are no water

Revolution 3

I have so many middle names Loaf
meet me tonight @five

Rush Hour Libation Square
leave your car on the highway

walk out walk slowly
start there!

Revolution 4

Had the tyrant put his madness
into writing

how would the story read if it were not told
slant

Democracy is that
a tyrant can't preside for life

Revolution 5

We daydream what we do not wake up from
in time to remember

We can't chant what the people want
some is not all

oneness is difference
art serves

Blake

wrote "Imagination has nothing
to do with Memory"

admits it is a bit harsh
Best-case scenario it pays

memory minimum wage
for pure recollection of data

Spring & All

When last poetry was for masses
you weren't born

that's what mass remembers if so
the mutable to each

spider a web
fiberoptics connects the dots

Darwish

If olive trees knew the hands that had planted
them
olive oil would have turned into tears!

Our names our body parts
I you

butterfly flutter
or swarm

"Neither for nor Against"

The live oak's been shaved
into a nude figure Walt

license of possessing
a new house

What's left of natives Walt?
Catalogs of names

Emily

I used to think you part Black or Wampa-
noag
those lips that nose

no dashes here auburn all burned
In his grave

Celan turns my name
tastes to me of sand

Portraits

Death is not our only betrayal
we are having technical difficulties

John so why don't you say
a few words to that effect

turning ashes
into berries

Arabic

calligraphy on train tracks
a pocket-size Quran asunder

sun-bleached rodent skeletons
my son & I skipping sleepers

listening to whistles
no train came

Revenge

is not what you're after you're after what
you cannot name but names you

Revenge is after you
After you

words be my body
lick my ears against revenge

My Funny Life

is one caboose after another
caboose in Arabic meaning nightmare

turned into a two-bedroom cabin
in a resort town

sunset & rise
eureka's Rothko

Textu

What's the idea?
No idea is an island

Whoview bin talking 2?
A fistula is an isthmus

Heavenchew an app for it?
We shed light then leave its husk behind

Translation

You live in a dream
biopsy is set within hours racemes

will bloom inside your flesh
in LaserJet graphic

or disseminate smudge
into transfigurines

Or

I'm abscess
A small state to subjugate the world

body the word body or
I touch plurality so much I become the just-one

Self-cell switch-cell
Communicative

Mutual Fund

I am tired of kissing you
once a month

Kindness held hostage
whose ransom is your death

You're already a book
on trees that flower hands & autumn

Fidelity

is a business deal
one secret slipping into another

I don't mean at the beach
we're above sea level

But echo in conch
Your heart needs a hearing aid

Luke Cool Hand I'm Your Father

Nurturing people into junkies
par for the course

pills & fear
& salt & sugar & grease

@the dollar store
They did have a choice

Softly killing them softly

@consumerist rates
science isn't final

on a few points
If you want to smear smear

just don't misconstrue me
I get paid well for it

& poets who get paid as much

wholly we listen to them
Don't get all Che on me cheri

my patients "my"
as if I own them

as long as they're nothing
but patients

& they me of course

they are called "lives"
This life loved you

that one got you a newsboy cap
gift card for fancy steak

or asked you to her house
or funeral

In tyranny there's also love

as gesture & as such
compassion is easy

a deductible or co-pay
or who'd do this calling

 "we-anoint-you-demigod"
a who's who club

As for mass murder

it doesn't need to occur
acutely in order

for it to be that
It's not the hell one enters

but the hell one enters others into
& also enters

Patient

I see you rolling your eyes in your grave!
you are up now

electronic record
step up to the plate

What we've had is an affair
we don't need a physical

He

is always building me
a pretty house up there in my dreams

my two legs back on me
I am ready to rejoin him

My tamales were once
served in the White House!

102

I laugh all the time to keep from crying!
Next B-day will be on the local news

My body's shifted my tears
to my nose

which makes
my great-grandson queasy

Time

It was last night in his sleep
You have helped him to the best two years

those toolshed days
Do you know for sure Doc

if your last words to him
were kind

87

This is no retirement
you have your body still

symptoms to report
visits to keep meds to refill

referrals bill after bill relapse recovery
full-time dying

Hospice Hymn

You live despite of what
we do to you not because of it

Stay home
keep our gadgets

We'll come when the going's tough
Letting go is in your hands

Window Has Closed

tolerating machine
much better since much more

gentle fluid removal you'll die
laughing or into a rage from feedback

coming by tonight
life

CHF

Rooster calls no one wakes
on time morphine veins

through no one's sleep the city's eternal
pump hour all is work is none

birds chirp endless
is the rain

Two Arrows

King Lear's daughters
wanted him revolving to hospital

they loved him so
He was kind no king old & tired of it all

they let him go
Some love kills

The One

who opened door for wolf now howls
with eyes that turn to ink

return to leather unbound
The one who's now fish-bird

bird-fish who now
some love kills

The Mind in State

Does consciousness exist
only when you name it?
Was the double helix a
stranger, the nucleus the
first brain? I feel therefore
I am. This is more
peptide than pep-talk.
The tongueless moon is
sticking its tongue out at
us. The mountain wool
is shaved into vineyards.
Without other there is no
self & we are not always
the others of other selves.
Is the moon a self, is wine
or grape? The body &
the as-if body, taking time
taste waking slow rain
healing grass.

Elegy for Neurotransmitters

1

Enough said
it's mirage's echo

of moderns who
repeat the scene already set in the script

of mind's office space
as mind ensnares

the outside in prisoner swap
of the inside need of self before art

poem's pretext
to keep the dead alive mummified

on ventilators
evolution's assembly lines

those dream mouth anachronisms
that diverticulate the brain in rest-

oration memory as imagination
ordered disordered

sedimentation rate out of hand
into it

2

So that the delta the self's
undisrupted flow lava & ana

& other as past & the past
no more than has forever

existed beyond word & pixel
consciousness will

at the synapse of a finger
in the cleft of reuptake

bits & bytes of I molecular
voice that is always there not always

sound or heard
pure messenger coursing

precursor shot depleted
in a world of non-I & gated action

potential which one of us
is the indigent endogenous source?

Your life
I must modulate your life!

Authenticity Bargain

I love you more than the world loves itself
the world doesn't love itself that much

Eternal sameness
divided by fleeting

Algebra's
zebra

Tomography

The world isn't good with names
can't place a face

without the histories of organs
states of teeth

particle & antiparticle
our mystic annihilation

When the Grandmother Dies

it'll be kept secret
from her four daughters

who'll be flying in
from three different countries

after years of absence
reunion ends

When the grandmother dies

it'll ruin summertime
for the grandkids who

in their mothers' grief will eat
okra each day

fresh & leftover
till it tastes like ash

When the grandmother dies

the groundskeeper will beg for cash
he comforts her he'll say

& the sisters
will reply

Were it not for you
the dead would have died

Syncope

To be alone with others
who are each alone is not to be

alone alone Pinocchio wolf
snow white lies in range of

satellite dish ear-snout
minstrel show

Kiss Pollution

In the hallucinatory gorge
my first two-lipped tulip

sheltered in night air
that withstood so much!

Little air that could
no longer sieve:

translation?

1st find corollary flower
whose name is mouth

then Tax Break
As when Omar asked a thief if he'd enough
to eat

Thief said No
Omar spared his hand

Martyrdom

Stop it with the we already
are mucosal tourette or
sublingual compliance.
It is Christmas. Even the
wretched survive indie
style. Did you get me my
dopamine fix to smooth
out my shuffle? You only
leave clipped fingernails in
my bed. I presume they're
yours. & Kleenex crumpled
& lost among the folds.
I'm going commando this
summer, hole in my sock
be darned. O duende that
gives me mass, feathered
time in a black hole, lit
years, dog years, god
years, pick a number.

Anonymous

People are a vast deep sea
Oh to be away from them

is a ship
& dearly beloved when I think of thee

I shudder like a wet sparrow
Graves don't thirst

Rain

We have entered the language of clouds
the weather is all over

Will you open your umbrella
or turn off the rain

We held our children's toys
in our hands

Saliva

for toothpaste 2 pees per flush
camaraderie with living under a bridge

sand water exfoliation
pail shower mug

weakest of faith
no one talks about shit

Believe

or disbelieve the massacre
took size & place it doesn't erase

the prerequisite preceding terror
Catastrophe

is not always evidence-based
Also erasure

Shock

Kill a squirrel with pellets
save the yard's cherry & green tomatoes

the heart is murky
like machine gun oil

clear all clear
a lidocaine-filled syringe

Awe

The little I knew then is not the little I know now
living among ruins

a fetish I have
no more fucks to give

larynxless
evidence doesn't speak for itself

Vigil

Prolife-ration to nuclear divide
prolife nation to pluripotent cell

criteria to treat
malnutrition

sometimes I wake up in bed on my knees
sleep-praying

You Cannot

go on neologizing forever always
from each book a page

is missing the ice-cream truck
its sirens & harem

of seals tongues in ear
don't odyssize me

Rubaiyat FitzGerald

Do you know why I like Persians?
an older veteran I was caring for

in the emergency room asked me
Why? I asked

Because they are not
Arabs

Captain America

Captain Boomer or Ahab
or the massless photon whose trespassing

rhythm wrong-foots me
I ain't no Queequeg's coffin

You already call me
Ismael

Right of Return

Body scan
of present-absent organ views

memory's polygraph
triumph over the paranoiac-critical method

star-nomad
searched for if reached gone

Dear Sister

a September is had
in Shatila a 14-year-old girl wrote

"My love I'm like a rose
some days I decorate weddings

other days graves"
She is not alone

Dear Sister

life is a conspiracy
As zygote

you were subaltern you couldn't speak
or you spoke when no one was listening

were spoken for when silent
a wedding

Dear Sister

in Phoenix an American woman has been
saving
Afghan women

& her French husband who helped
in the kitchen said

The Congolese fathom
only violence!

Cockroach

climbed in my mouth & out
cockroach in my ear drummed me

Cockroach lipids on shoe sole
& scalded in kitchen sink

Lizards bleed
patience of ushering

33

If not by the sword then by other means
means are many & death is one

Those whom you love are gone
& like a sword you remain alone

a light
or its skeleton

Thank You Dark World

If not for you there'd be
among other things no poetry

no silken boredom
"only triumphal songs

of spreading happiness"
I would like that

I Only Want from Love

That poetry makes nothing happen
nothing 2 makes poetry happen

nothing is nothing can come
of nothing comes

to mind we
are late for now

A Word in Arabic

sends you a word returns you
or leads you to the spring

& brings you back thirsty
You can tile the ocean floor

plaster heaven
69 is 78 or 87

The Old Man Who Wept

this morning in the clinic room
for himself & his wife

of 62 years
let me hold his hand

for 7 minutes as he wept & suffered
chronic love

Each now competed

to care for the other & deter
the other from the illness

of caring
while hiding behind names

the body gives & is given
hearts kidneys lungs

Their children are around

& wonderful yet the couple
knows they will go it alone

For 4 summers
he's shared with me

a basketful of lemons
from his lemon trees

The bees

we have talked about them
How sometimes the trees

will bear twice in a year
how my single lemon tree

turned out to be exactly
like the ones he grows

When he dies

if he dies before me I won't go to his funeral
I won't know his wife

If she dies first
I'd help him hurry waiting

hold his hand again
for longer

I am going out to my tree now

that it has finally borne
bent low this year

beautiful kyphotic
I'll share with him

my lemons
Please come back for 1 visit more

In Love

patience is in need of patience a stroke
of the imagination unspeakable

a vanishing joy
banished to joy

not insomnia not sleep
& knowing when you die

I Come

into the shadow of a shadow
I thieve myself

return to the scene of thyme
inside you the map of days plays

itself out fast times
olive oil bread breath

The river of fear

isn't that of desire
your eye-

lashes a crescent a crescent
shines on snow you

fractal star of my eye repeat nerve fire
firing when we come

My heart pounds

your lips
as if I have been chewing on foxglove

by the side of the road or in a meadow
There're flowers for ruins

or forensics
& there's this

A History

In glass shower stall erect
I lean on you your back to me we let

curvature & angle be
a cat readying fluff for sleep

a cat nap's where
we're headed

or a rub before rubbing

a border at the limits of visa
or watching you arrive

without touching
you directly or indirectly

or as far as being
watched is touch

Of Your Lovers Who

I roll my dough I roll my dough
to the memory of you my sugar-

cane milk I roll my cane
to the memory of you

I roll & roll
my milky dough!

Travelling Light

Distance dissolves as distance
place as place

In you I'm near & far
& I in me is what you are

but near myself I'm not
myself so just how far

Tie Me Up

to the sea pebbles of your fingers
I'm no boat or Houdini

to release myself my dappled skin
to your tongue's labors

once a sea shores up
its debris

It's true

the farther I stand from you
the better you look

Like Monet's lilies
Better isn't the word clearer is

Better for me is
the indecipherable proximity

Tie me up

without metaphor & unlimited to my body
time me up incorporated

my consumered organism
mind soul etc.

All that that times me up
while you tie me up

Dancing

Frisked breath
the dovetailed glass unravels

in the heart laughter falls
on our bodies we kiss

the way desert refuses rain
from the sky or into earth

Arc de Triomphe

Two lover trees
two pecans in a field

or maybe twins who sustained
the same height & chiral joined at the top

parading wind
sheltering cattle

Textu

Your spine a river into the forest
can't tell the neurons for the trees

I light & light
you up with sound profile

threading the image habit
of pleasure

Conscience

When we learn how an infant in the womb
sleeps precisely in a parent's pose

say with fist closed
pillowing the temple

What will become
of the poem

About the Author

Fady Joudah's *The Earth in the Attic* was selected for the Yale Series of Younger Poets. His awards and honors include a Banipal Prize for Arabic Literary Translation, a PEN Center USA Literary Award, and a 2013 Griffin Poetry Prize for his translation of *Like a Straw Bird It Follows Me, and Other Poems* by Ghassan Zaqtan. He is a doctor of internal medicine in Houston, Texas.

Poetry is vital to language and living. Since 1972, Copper Canyon Press has published extraordinary poetry from around the world to engage the imaginations and intellects of readers, writers, booksellers, librarians, teachers, students, and donors.